COBBLERS,
CRISPS,
and
DEEP-DISH PIES

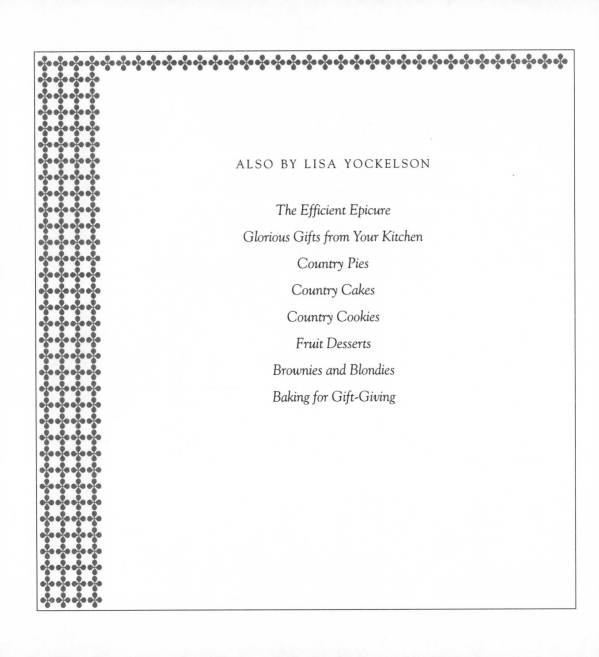

ALSO BY LISA YOCKELSON

The Efficient Epicure

Glorious Gifts from Your Kitchen

Country Pies

Country Cakes

Country Cookies

Fruit Desserts

Brownies and Blondies

Baking for Gift-Giving

American Baking Classics

COBBLERS, CRISPS,
and
DEEP-DISH PIES

LISA YOCKELSON

HarperCollins*Publishers*

HarperCollins books may be purchased for educational, business, or sales promotional use. For information please write: Special Markets Department, HarperCollins Publishers, Inc., 10 East 53rd Street, New York, NY 10022.

FIRST EDITION

Designed by Helene Wald Berinsky

Library of Congress Cataloging-in-Publication Data

Yockelson, Lisa
Cobblers, crisps, and deep-dish pies / Lisa Yockelson—1st ed.
p.   cm.—(American baking classics)
ISBN: 0-06-016749-1
1. Desserts.   2. Cookery (Fruit)   I. Title.   II. Series.
TX773.Y627   1995
641.8'15—dc20   94-23771

95 96 97 98 99 ❖/RRD 10 9 8 7 6 5 4 3 2 1

ACKNOWLEDGMENTS

Thoughtful guidance from Susan Lescher, my literary agent, and Susan Friedland, my editor at HarperCollins Publishers (who must adore fruit desserts, for it was she who suggested that I write a book full of cobblers, crisps, and pies), has brought this baking book to completion. Also at HarperCollins, Joseph Montebello, Creative Director, continues to compose such attractive volumes out of my prose and recipes; Jennifer Griffin, Assistant Editor, follows the book to completion with diligence; and Wende Gozan, Publicist, offers kind and unlimited support when a new book finally makes it way onto the shelves in stores far and wide.

And what would a cookbook author do without a cluster of friends willing to taste, judge, contrast, compare, and recommend, to go raspberry- and blackberry-picking on blazing summer afternoons, to drive long distances in pursuit of just one more harvest of cooking apples? To all of those who have shared these moments in time with me—on gravel roads, in the kitchen, and around the table—my thanks. Certainly you know who you are.

Contents

Introduction

SAVORING FRUIT DESSERTS

Deeply rooted in the tradition of American cooking, the baking of cobblers, crisps, and deep-dish pies makes good use of the seasonal yield gathered from the orchard and garden. Typically, these desserts are made from a generous amount of fruit, sugared and spiced just enough to bring out their natural flavor, before they are topped off with a covering—a biscuit dough, a crumble of flour, butter, sugar, and nuts, or a sheath of pastry. Once baked, what you have is a sweet made up of succulent fruit protected by a crisp, tender, or flaky lid.

The baked fruit desserts in this volume are fresh-tasting and delectable. They look homemade and handcrafted, and those two qualities make them uncommonly inviting. Ideally, cobblers, crisps, and deep-dish pies are best served warm (bake them on the very day that they're to be eaten), when their full taste can be appreciated, though pies and crisps, in particular, are certainly just as good when served barely warm or at room temperature. They can be enjoyed all year round, with or without such accompaniments as a custard or yogurt sauce.

Cobblers

By design, a cobbler is a home-style pudding consisting of a layer of sweetened fruit covered by a topping of biscuit dough, practically taking on the appearance of a deep-dish pie. The resemblance is close enough that it prompts culinary historians to link the cobbler to a deep-dish pie: John F. Mariani, author of *The Dictionary of American Food and Drink* (New Haven and New York: Ticknor and Fields, 1983), defines the cobbler as "a western deep-dish pie with a thick crust and a fruit filling."

The layer of fruit—be it berries, sliced fruit, dried fruit, or any thoughtful combination of the three—is generally bolstered by a sweetening agent (granulated or superfine sugar, light or dark brown sugar, a fruit syrup, honey, jam, jelly, marmalade, maple syrup, and the like), sometimes tinged with spices (such as ground cinnamon, freshly grated nutmeg, or pinches of cardamom, ginger, or allspice) or grated citrus peel, notably lemon or orange.

The soft fruits and berries of summer, such as peaches, plums, nectarines, blueberries, and blackberries, give off a certain amount of liquid while baking, so cobblers made with juicy specimens need to be *lightly* thickened with flour and cornstarch. Thoroughly combining the thickener with the sugar and spices, or slaking it with a spoonful of fruit juice or water before tossing it with the fruit, creates a lovely slightly condensed "sauce" that clings gently to the slices of fruit or berries when baked.

Another important reason to thicken watery fruit for cobbler making is that the biscuit covering needs a substantial foundation. Lacking that, the mounds of dough would absorb too much liquid and would bake up pasty, sodden, and messy. The generous amount of fruit used in deep-dish pies also needs to be thickened to keep the pastry cover crisp and firm. One word of advice: The amount of cornstarch or flour suggested in the recipes that follow is based on using *ripe* fruit or berries. You might have to tinker with that quantity. One means of determining the juiciness of the fruit is to look at the bottom of the bowl containing the cut-up fruit. If more than a tablespoon of liquid settles at the bottom of the mixing bowl, do use the full amount of thickener. And you can be sure that a few cups of berries, while not trickling out much liquid on mixing with sugar and spices, will be sure to exude plenty of juice when exposed to the oven's intense heat; thus, I encourage you to use sufficient flour or cornstarch when working with berries alone or in combination with sliced fruit.

A biscuit dough, the traditional cobbler topping, can be made in two ways—in mounds spooned over the fruit, or rolled and cut into circles, then placed, overlapping, to partially cover the fruit. The softer dough, similar to a drop biscuit dough but slightly richer, is either spooned into nicely shaped heaps or spread into a rough cover. The biscuit rounds, made from dough rolled or patted onto a work surface and stamped out with a cookie cutter, are placed over the fruit; this look resembles cobblestones, which give the rustic sweet its name.

I favor a drop biscuit dough because it is the fastest and easiest of the two, and because the texture is supremely lighter and a dash more cake-like. The method for creating the softer dough is described on the next page.

Just before baking, dust the top of the cobbler with granulated sugar to give it a golden appearance and a feathery, sweet crunch.

With a helping of cobbler, offer good vanilla ice cream, a hand-stirred, stovetop-cooked custard (such as the one on page 80), or—and this is a personal favorite—just a pouring of preservative-free heavy cream, plain and simple.

Vanilla-Scented Biscuit Topping

• *Enough drop biscuit dough to cover a 9- to 10-inch dish of fruit* •

*L*ight and tender, this easily mixed biscuit dough is raised with baking powder and flavored with vanilla extract. The liquid used to bind the dry ingredients is milk, although light cream (or "top milk" as it was called in the past) is a richer substitute for whole milk. For that indulgent, old-time taste, switch over to light cream and consider using that variation when mixing the dough for a peach, blueberry, or blackberry cobbler.

1½ cups unsifted all-purpose flour
2 teaspoons baking powder
⅛ teaspoon salt
3 tablespoons cold unsalted butter, cubed

3 tablespoons shortening
2 tablespoons granulated sugar
¾ cup milk blended with 1½ teaspoons vanilla extract

Whisk together the flour, baking powder, and salt in a large mixing bowl. Add the cubes of butter and shortening and, using two table knives, cut the butter into small dime-size bits. Crumble the flour and butter mixture between your fingertips until the texture resembles coarse-cut oatmeal, leaving the fat in small pearl-size lumps. Stir in the granulated sugar. Stir in the milk-vanilla blend. The consistency of the dough should be medium-firm and soft, slightly fluffy and sticky, and, when scooped up in a spoon, should hold its shape.

Drop heaping tablespoons of dough (there will be about 10 to 12 in total) over the prepared fruit, leaving gaps here and there. The mounds will puff up slightly on baking, sometimes melding together in spots, and that is what makes the look of the cobbler so appealing. Bake the cobbler as directed in each recipe.

VARIATIONS

For *Spiced Vanilla-Scented Biscuit Topping*, whisk ¼ teaspoon ground cinnamon, ¼ teaspoon freshly grated nutmeg, and ⅛ teaspoon ground allspice into the flour mixture with the baking powder and salt.

For *Vanilla-Scented Biscuit Topping with Currants*, stir 2 tablespoons moist, dried currants into the flour-butter mixture along with the granulated sugar.

For *Vanilla-Scented Biscuit Topping with Nuts*, stir ¼ cup chopped walnuts, pecans, or almonds into the flour-butter mixture along with the granulated sugar.

Apple Cobbler with Raisins and Walnuts

• *6 servings* •

The flavor of this cobbler is reminiscent of apple strudel, with a light seasoning of aromatic spices and a toss of raisins and walnuts.

5 cooking apples (about 1⅔ pounds), peeled, cored, and sliced
1 tablespoon lemon juice
½ cup superfine sugar blended with 1 teaspoon ground cinnamon, ½ teaspoon freshly grated nutmeg, and a pinch of ground allspice

2 tablespoons dark raisins
3 tablespoons chopped walnuts
1 recipe Vanilla-Scented Biscuit Topping (page 6)
About 2 teaspoons granulated sugar

Preheat the oven to 425 degrees. Butter a 9- to 10-inch oval oven-proof baking dish that is 3 inches deep.

In a mixing bowl, toss the apples with the lemon juice. Sprinkle over the superfine sugar-spice blend, mix well, and let stand for 5 minutes. Fold the raisins and walnuts through this. Spoon the fruit and nut mixture into the baking dish.

Drop heaping tablespoons of the biscuit topping over the fruit. Sprinkle the granulated sugar over the biscuit topping.

Bake the cobbler for 10 minutes. Reduce the oven temperature to 400 degrees and continue baking for 40 minutes longer, or until the apples are tender and the topping is golden.

VARIATION

For *Apple Cobbler with Dried Cherries and Walnuts,* substitute 3 tablespoons coarsely chopped sweet dried cherries for the raisins.

Peach-Blueberry Cobbler

• *6 servings* •

*W*hen peaches and blueberries are good and plentiful, they need little in the way of enhancement to make a luscious cobbler—with the sugar, just add a squeeze of lemon juice, flecks of lemon peel, and a dash of cinnamon.

5 peaches (about 1¼ pounds), peeled, pitted, and sliced
1 cup blueberries, picked over
2 teaspoons lemon juice
1 teaspoon grated lemon peel
⅓ cup superfine sugar (or more to taste) blended with 2¾ teaspoons cornstarch and ¼ teaspoon ground cinnamon

1½ tablespoons unsalted butter, melted and cooled
1 recipe Vanilla-Scented Biscuit Topping (page 6)

Preheat the oven to 425 degrees. Butter a 9- to 10-inch oval ovenproof baking dish that is 3 inches deep.

In a mixing bowl, toss the peaches and blueberries with the lemon juice, lemon peel, and superfine sugar-cornstarch-cinnamon blend. Let stand for 5 minutes. Spoon the fruit into the baking dish. Drizzle the butter over the fruit.

Drop heaping tablespoons of the biscuit topping over the fruit.

Bake the cobbler for 10 minutes. Reduce the oven temperature to 400 degrees and continue baking for about 35 minutes longer, or until the fruit is bubbly and the topping is golden.

Fresh and Dried Cherry Cobbler

• *6 servings* •

Serve this cobbler, full of the bright and intense tang of both fresh and dried cherries, with plain vanilla ice cream.

3½ cups cherries (about 1¾
    pounds), pitted
3 tablespoons dried pitted
    cherries
¼ teaspoon almond extract
⅓ cup red currant jelly, warmed
    until melted down
2 tablespoons granulated sugar
    blended with 2 teaspoons
    cornstarch, ¼ teaspoon
    ground cinnamon, and
    ¼ teaspoon ground allspice

2 tablespoons unsalted butter,
    melted and cooled
1 recipe Spiced Vanilla-Scented
    Biscuit Topping (page 7)

Preheat the oven to 425 degrees. Butter a 9- to 10-inch oval oven-proof baking dish that is 3 inches deep.

In a mixing bowl, toss the fresh cherries, dried cherries, almond extract, jelly, and granulated sugar-cornstarch-spice blend. Let stand for 5 minutes. Spoon the fruit into the baking dish. Drizzle the butter over the fruit.

Drop heaping tablespoons of the biscuit topping over the fruit.

Bake the cobbler for 10 minutes. Reduce the oven temperature to 400 degrees and continue baking for about 35 to 40 minutes longer, or until the cherries are tender and the topping is golden.

Blackberry Cobbler

• 6 servings •

During the summertime, I convert hand-picked quarts of brilliant, plump blackberries into a choice cobbler, sweetened just so with both sugar and a small amount of blackberry jam. It's simple and regal.

3½ cups blackberries, picked
over
¼ cup blackberry jam, warmed
until melted down
½ cup superfine sugar blended
with 2 teaspoons cornstarch
and ½ teaspoon ground
cinnamon

1 teaspoon grated lemon peel
2 tablespoons unsalted butter, melted
and cooled
1 recipe Vanilla-Scented Biscuit
Topping (page 6)

Preheat the oven to 425 degrees. Butter a 9- to 10-inch oval ovenproof baking dish that is 3 inches deep.

In a mixing bowl, toss the blackberries with the jam, superfine sugar-cornstarch-cinnamon blend, and lemon peel. Let stand for 5 minutes. Spoon the fruit into the baking dish. Drizzle the butter over the fruit.

Drop heaping tablespoons of the biscuit topping over the fruit.

Bake the cobbler for 10 minutes. Reduce the oven temperature to 400 degrees and continue baking for about 35 minutes longer, or until the blackberries are bubbly and the topping is golden.

Orange-Rhubarb Cobbler

• 6 servings •

*T*he marmalade softens the tartness of the rhubarb, and the orange juice adds another subtle fruity taste to this cobbler.

8 stalks trimmed and sliced
    rhubarb (about 4 cups)
⅓ cup orange juice
½ cup orange marmalade
⅓ cup superfine sugar blended
    with 2¾ teaspoons cornstarch
    and ¼ teaspoon ground
    allspice
1 teaspoon grated orange peel

1 recipe Vanilla-Scented Biscuit
    Topping (page 6)
    or
1 recipe Vanilla-Scented Biscuit
    Topping with Currants (page 7)
    or
1 recipe Vanilla-Scented Biscuit
    Topping with Nuts (page 7),
    using walnuts or pecans

Preheat the oven to 425 degrees. Butter a 9- to 10-inch oval oven-proof baking dish that is 3 inches deep.

In a mixing bowl, toss the rhubarb with the orange juice, marmalade, superfine sugar-cornstarch-allspice blend, and orange peel. Let stand for 5 minutes. Spoon the fruit into the baking dish.

Drop heaping tablespoons of the biscuit topping over the fruit.

Bake the cobbler for 10 minutes. Reduce the oven temperature to 400 degrees and continue baking for about 35 to 40 minutes longer, or until the rhubarb is tender and the topping is golden.

NOTE: At the market, rhubarb is generally sold trimmed of its leaves, which are poisonous and should never be consumed or used in baking.

Pear Cobbler with Dates

• *6 servings* •

*T*his is an earthy, country-style cobbler. The dates, blended into a coarse puree with pear nectar, along with the maple syrup, flatter the taste of the sliced pears. For the cobbler, use firm but ripe d'Anjou pears.

¼ cup chopped pitted dates
¼ cup pear nectar
5 pears (about 1⅔ pounds),
    peeled, cored, and sliced
¼ teaspoon freshly grated nutmeg
¼ teaspoon ground cinnamon
⅓ cup maple syrup
1 tablespoon unsalted butter,
    melted and cooled

1 recipe Vanilla-Scented Biscuit
    Topping (page 6)
    or
1 recipe Vanilla-Scented Biscuit
    Topping with Nuts (page 7),
    using walnuts

Preheat the oven to 425 degrees. Butter a 9- to 10-inch oval oven-proof baking dish that is 3 inches deep.

Puree the dates and pear nectar in the bowl of a food processor fitted with the steel blade. Scrape the date mixture into a mixing bowl and combine with the pears, nutmeg, cinnamon, and maple syrup. Spoon the fruit into the baking dish. Drizzle the butter over the fruit.

Drop heaping tablespoons of the biscuit topping over the fruit.

Bake the cobbler for 10 minutes. Reduce the oven temperature to 400 degrees and continue baking for about 35 minutes longer, or until the pears are tender and the topping is golden.

Gingered Nectarine Cobbler

• *6 servings* •

*A*s a variation of this cobbler, use peaches in place of the nectarines and accent the fruit mixture with a tablespoon of peach jam in addition to the preserved ginger.

6 nectarines (about 1½ pounds), halved, pitted, and sliced
2 tablespoons golden raisins, coarsely chopped
¼ cup apricot jam
3 tablespoons granulated sugar blended with 1½ teaspoons cornstarch and ¼ teaspoon ground ginger

1 tablespoon chopped ginger preserved in syrup
1 tablespoon unsalted butter, melted and cooled
1 recipe Vanilla-Scented Biscuit Topping (page 6)

Preheat the oven to 425 degrees. Butter a 9- to 10-inch oval oven-proof baking dish that is 3 inches deep.

In a mixing bowl, toss the nectarines and raisins with the jam, granulated sugar-cornstarch-ginger blend, and preserved ginger. Let stand for 5 minutes. Spoon the fruit into the baking dish. Drizzle the butter over the fruit.

Drop heaping tablespoons of the biscuit topping over the fruit.

Bake the cobbler for 10 minutes. Reduce the oven temperature to 400 degrees and continue baking for about 35 minutes longer, or until the nectarines are tender and the topping is golden.

❖❖❖❖❖❖

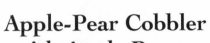

Apple-Pear Cobbler
with Apple Butter

• *6 servings* •

*T*his is a down-to-earth, wholesome cobbler that combines a few superb staples of the fall baking kitchen—apples, pears, apple butter, and apple cider. In the cobbler, using Empire, Cortland, or Stayman apples and d'Anjou pears produces a dessert with the best flavor and texture. Serve with a silky pouring custard, such as the Nutmeg Custard Sauce on page 80.

3 cooking apples (about
    1 pound), peeled, cored,
    and sliced
3 pears (about 1 pound), peeled,
    cored, and sliced
1 teaspoon lemon juice
¼ cup apple butter blended with
    ¼ cup apple cider and 3
    tablespoons granulated sugar

2 tablespoons unsalted butter or
    margarine, melted and cooled
1 recipe Vanilla-Scented Biscuit
    Topping (page 6)
    or
1 recipe Spiced Vanilla-Scented
    Biscuit Topping (page 7)

Preheat the oven to 425 degrees. Butter a 9- to 10-inch oval oven-proof baking dish that is 3 inches deep.

In a mixing bowl, toss the apples and pears with the lemon juice and apple butter-cider-granulated sugar blend. Let stand for 5 minutes. Spoon the fruit into the baking dish. Drizzle the butter over the fruit.

Drop heaping tablespoons of the biscuit topping over the fruit.

Bake the cobbler for 10 minutes. Reduce the oven temperature to 400 degrees and continue baking for about 35 minutes longer, or until the fruit is tender and the topping is golden.

Peach Cobbler with
Dried Strawberries and Rum

• *6 servings* •

*T*his elegant cobbler blends a mixture of succulent sliced peaches and dried strawberries that are trickled with light rum. Dried strawberries have a marvelous concentrated flavor; they are at once mellow, fruity, and sweet. I love to have them on hand in the larder for adding to (and perking up) fresh fruit compotes and pies. Dried strawberries also mix favorably with nectarines, cherries, plums, apples, and pears.

¼ cup dried strawberries,
 coarsely chopped
2 tablespoons light rum
6 peaches (about 1½ pounds),
 peeled, halved, pitted, and
 sliced
⅓ cup granulated sugar blended
 with 1 tablespoon cornstarch
 and ¼ teaspoon ground
 allspice

2 teaspoons lemon juice
1 tablespoon unsalted butter, melted
 and cooled
1 recipe Vanilla-Scented Biscuit
 Topping (page 6)
2 teaspoons granulated sugar

Preheat the oven to 425 degrees. Butter a 9- to 10-inch oval oven-proof baking dish that is 3 inches deep.

Place the strawberries in a small bowl, pour over the rum, and let stand for 10 to 15 minutes. In a mixing bowl, toss the peaches with the granulated sugar-cornstarch-allspice blend and lemon juice. Let stand for 5 minutes. Add the strawberries and rum. Toss again. Spoon the fruit into the baking dish. Drizzle the butter over the fruit.

Drop heaping tablespoons of the biscuit topping over the fruit. Sprinkle the granulated sugar over the biscuit topping.

Bake the cobbler for 10 minutes. Reduce the oven temperature to 400 degrees and continue baking for about 35 minutes longer, or until the peaches are tender and bubbly and the topping is golden.

Red Plum–Dried Cranberry Cobbler

• *6 servings* •

$\mathcal{D}$ried cranberries, although not as sharp as the fresh variety, have a concentrated fruit flavor and complement many of the soft fruits, especially plums, peaches, and nectarines.

10 red plums (about 2 pounds), halved, pitted, and sliced

¼ cup dried cranberries, coarsely chopped

⅓ cup granulated sugar blended with ¼ teaspoon ground cinnamon

2 teaspoons cornstarch dissolved in 2 tablespoons cranberry juice (or substitute unsweetened apple juice)

1 tablespoon unsalted butter, melted and cooled

1 recipe Vanilla-Scented Biscuit Topping (page 6)

or

1 recipe Vanilla-Scented Biscuit Topping with Nuts (page 7), using walnuts

Preheat the oven to 425 degrees. Butter a 9- to 10-inch oval ovenproof baking dish that is 3 inches deep.

In a mixing bowl, toss the plums and cranberries with the granulated sugar-cinnamon mixture and the cornstarch-juice blend. Let stand for 5 minutes. Spoon the fruit into the baking dish. Drizzle the butter over the fruit.

Drop heaping tablespoons of the biscuit topping over the fruit.

Bake the cobbler for 10 minutes. Reduce the oven temperature to 400 degrees and continue baking for about 30 to 35 minutes longer, or until the plums are tender and bubbly and the topping is golden.

❖❖❖❖❖

Apple-Mincemeat Cobbler

• *6 servings* •

$\mathcal{S}$everal dollops of glistening all-fruit mincemeat do wonders for the taste of apples that are sliced and baked in a cobbler. If homemade mincemeat is unavailable, chop up a small handful of dried fruit (such as apricots, peaches, cherries, and pears), moisten with a little apple juice and a few teaspoons of brandy or apple cider, and use that in place of the mincemeat.

5 cooking apples (about 1⅔
pounds), peeled, cored, and
sliced
⅓ cup plus 1 tablespoon Quick
Dried Fruit Mincemeat
(page 50)
2 teaspoons granulated sugar

½ teaspoon grated lemon peel
2 teaspoons lemon juice
1½ tablespoons unsalted butter,
melted and cooled
1 recipe Vanilla-Scented Biscuit
Topping (page 6)

Preheat the oven to 425 degrees. Butter a 9- to 10-inch oval oven-proof baking dish that is 3 inches deep.

In a mixing bowl, toss the apples with the mincemeat, granulated sugar, lemon peel, and lemon juice. Let stand for 5 minutes. Spoon the fruit into the baking dish. Drizzle the butter over the fruit.

Drop heaping tablespoons of the biscuit topping over the fruit.

Bake the cobbler for 10 minutes. Reduce the oven temperature to 400 degrees and continue baking for about 35 to 40 minutes longer, or until the apples are tender and the topping is golden.

❖❖❖❖❖

Apricot Cobbler

• *6 servings* •

*T*he fruit layer of this cobbler is made up of fresh apricots sweetened with a mixture of peach preserves and apple juice, and spiked with chopped dried peaches for tartness. If you happen to have a small, ripe peach on hand, puree it in a blender (or food processor) with the preserves and juice—this will add a lovely fragrance to the baked dessert.

12 fresh apricots (about 2 pounds), halved, pitted, and sliced

¼ cup dried peaches, coarsely chopped

½ cup peach preserves blended with ¼ cup unsweetened apple juice, 1¼ teaspoons ground cinnamon, ¼ teaspoon freshly grated nutmeg, and 2½ teaspoons cornstarch

2 teaspoons lemon juice

2 tablespoons unsalted butter, melted and cooled

1 recipe Vanilla-Scented Biscuit Topping (page 6)

or

1 recipe Spiced Vanilla-Scented Biscuit Topping (page 7)

Preheat the oven to 425 degrees. Butter a 9- to 10-inch oval oven-proof baking dish that is 3 inches deep.

In a mixing bowl, toss the fresh apricots and dried peaches with the peach preserves-juice-spice mixture and lemon juice. Let stand for 5 minutes. Spoon the fruit into the baking dish. Drizzle the butter over the fruit.

Drop heaping tablespoons of the biscuit topping over the fruit.

Bake the cobbler for 10 minutes. Reduce the oven temperature to 400 degrees and continue baking for about 35 minutes longer, or until the apricots are tender and the topping is golden.

Blueberry Cobbler with Glazed Lemon Peel

• *6 servings* •

*L*ightly glazed lemon peel, cut into irregular pieces, brightens the taste of the baked blueberries. Serve the cobbler with scoops of tangy lemon ice cream or Softly Whipped Cream (page 78).

10 thin strips lemon peel
¼ cup granulated sugar
½ cup water
3¾ cups blueberries, picked over
½ cup superfine sugar (or to taste) blended with 2¾ teaspoons cornstarch and ¼ teaspoon ground cinnamon

1 tablespoon unsalted butter, melted and cooled
1 recipe Vanilla-Scented Biscuit Topping (page 6)

Preheat the oven to 425 degrees. Butter a 9- to 10-inch oval oven-proof baking dish that is 3 inches deep.

Place the lemon peel in a nonreactive saucepan (preferably enameled cast iron) and add about 2 cups cold water. Bring to a boil, boil 1 minute, and drain. Repeat the process twice more.

Place the granulated sugar and ½ cup water in a small, nonreactive saucepan, cover, and cook over low heat until the sugar dissolves completely. Uncover, add the lemon peel, and cook slowly until the peel is tender, about 10 minutes. Using a slotted spoon, remove the peel to a side dish. When the peel is cool, chop it coarsely.

In a mixing bowl, toss the blueberries with the superfine sugar-cornstarch-cinnamon blend. Fold the lemon peel through the fruit. Let stand for 5 minutes. Spoon the fruit into the baking dish. Drizzle the butter over the fruit.

Drop heaping tablespoons of the biscuit topping over the fruit.

Bake the cobbler for 10 minutes. Reduce the oven temperature to 400 degrees and continue baking for about 35 minutes longer, or until the blueberries are bubbly and the topping is golden.

Crisps

A fruit crisp, an ideal fast-from-scratch dessert, gets its name from that crumbly mixture of flour, nuts, sugar, and butter that bakes into a crunchy cover over a few inches of fruit. Sometimes rolled oats or granola are used along with the flour to produce a heartier, but just as scrumptious, variation.

Usually the fruit for this dessert is sweetened lightly, to allow the natural flavors to dominate. Jams, jellies, and preserves (warmed slightly to liquefy), fruit syrups, and maple syrup are all fine substitutions for the granulated sugar, superfine sugar, or light brown sugar. A few drops of lemon juice heighten the taste of less than perfect fruit, as does finely grated citrus peel and dicings of glazed or dried fruit.

Most crisp toppings are made by introducing chunks of unsalted butter into the other ingredients to create soft, irregular flakes, using a pastry blender or two table knives to cut in the butter. The technique is identical to working fat into flour when making a pie crust. The flakes are combined further with the fingertips in order to turn a rough-hewn, almost sandy-looking, mixture into small lumps. This is scattered over the sliced fruit or berries and sent forth into the oven to bake. On baking, the top of the dessert will be golden and firm, and the fruit tender and bubbling.

Spoon the warm crisp, with its fragrant bouquet, into shallow bowls and serve very plain, or with small scoops of ice cream, a cascade of lightly sweetened whipped cream, or vanilla-flavored yogurt mixed with a drizzle of honey.

TOPPINGS FOR FRUIT CRISPS

Toppings for fruit crisps consist of standard pantry and refrigerator staples—flour, rolled oats, sugar, spices, butter, and, often, chopped nuts. Over the years, I have found that the key to making a superior topping depends on how well you combine the butter with the dry ingredients. Initially, the cubes of butter should be blended into the flour mixture with the help of two round-bladed table knives; the knives make easy work of cutting the butter into small bits. Once the butter is scattered throughout the mixture in little dabs, boldly press and crumble everything together with your fingertips, creating lumps both large and small. It is important to work the topping until these lumps are formed, for that is what creates a firm and, later, golden topping as the dessert bakes.

Any of the three toppings that follow can be made up to a day in advance and kept covered in the refrigerator. Always scatter the topping over the fruit in an even layer.

Nut Crisp Topping

• *Enough topping to cover a 9- to 10-inch dish of fruit* •

This good, all-purpose topping is a simple mixture of flour, sugar, spices, butter, and chopped nuts. If you are making a fruit crisp out of apples, pears, red or prune plums, or blackberries, walnuts in the topping would complement the fruit; for apricots, peaches, and cherries, choose almonds or macadamia nuts; and for blueberries or rhubarb, use pecans.

1 cup unsifted all-purpose flour
½ cup light brown sugar
3 tablespoons granulated sugar
½ teaspoon ground cinnamon
¼ teaspoon freshly grated nutmeg

8 tablespoons (1 stick) cold unsalted
  butter, cut into cubes
¾ cup chopped walnuts, pecans,
  almonds, or macadamia nuts

Mix the flour, light brown sugar, granulated sugar, cinnamon, and nutmeg in a mixing bowl. Scatter over the cubes of butter and, using two table knives, reduce the butter to small bits. Add the nuts. Blend all of the ingredients thoroughly with your fingertips until the mixture holds together in large, curdlike lumps.

Use the topping as directed in each recipe.

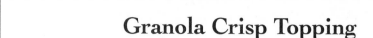

Granola Crisp Topping

• Enough topping to cover a 9- to 10-inch dish of fruit •

The firm, craggy quality of granola creates a crunchier topping than plain rolled oats would. This topping is especially pleasing when matched with such summer fruits as plums, peaches, or nectarines.

1¼ cups granola (without
    raisins)
¾ cup all-purpose flour
⅓ cup light brown sugar
¼ cup granulated sugar

½ teaspoon ground cinnamon
½ teaspoon freshly grated nutmeg
8 tablespoons (1 stick) cold unsalted
    butter, cut into cubes

Mix the granola, flour, light brown sugar, granulated sugar, cinnamon, and nutmeg in a mixing bowl. Scatter over the cubes of butter and, using two table knives, reduce the butter to small bits. Blend all of the ingredients thoroughly with your fingertips until the mixture holds together in large, curdlike lumps.

Use the topping as directed in each recipe.

Oatmeal Crisp Topping

• Enough topping to cover a 9- to 10-inch dish of fruit •

$\mathcal{U}$sing "old-fashioned" rolled oats seems to produce a sturdier topping than the "quick-cooking" variety.

1½ cups "old-fashioned" rolled
    oats
½ cup all-purpose flour
½ cup light brown sugar
¼ cup granulated sugar

1 teaspoon ground cinnamon
¼ teaspoon ground allspice
8 tablespoons (1 stick) cold unsalted
    butter, cut into cubes

Combine the oats, flour, light brown sugar, granulated sugar, cinnamon, and allspice in a bowl. Scatter over the cubes of butter and, using two table knives, reduce the butter to small bits. Blend all of the ingredients thoroughly with your fingertips until the mixture holds together in large, curdlike lumps.

Use the topping as directed in each recipe.

Pear Crisp with Bourbon and Maple Syrup

• 6 servings •

*I*n this crisp, the pears are sweetened with maple syrup rather than granulated sugar—the syrup gives an illusion of richness to the finished dessert. Ripe d'Anjou pears lend a perfumelike fruitiness to the dessert, but very ripe Bosc pears can be used as well. Softly Whipped Cream (see page 78) would be a splendid accompaniment.

6 pears (about 2 pounds),
   peeled, cored, and sliced
⅓ cup maple syrup
2 tablespoons bourbon
¼ teaspoon freshly grated nutmeg
¼ teaspoon ground cinnamon

1 recipe Nut Crisp Topping
   (page 34), made with walnuts
or
1 recipe Oatmeal Crisp Topping
   (page 36)

Preheat the oven to 375 degrees. Butter a 9-inch oval ovenproof baking dish.

In a mixing bowl, toss the pears with the maple syrup, bourbon, nutmeg, and cinnamon. Spoon the fruit into the baking dish. Sprinkle the crisp topping over the fruit in an even layer.

Bake the crisp for 40 to 45 minutes, or until the pears are tender and the topping is golden.

Apricot-Almond Crisp

• *6 servings* •

*R*ipe, fresh apricots give slightly to the touch, and their perfumelike essence is enhanced by poaching or baking in a pie, cobbler, or crisp. Ground cinnamon adds a mild spicy flavor to the fruit.

12 fresh apricots (about 2 pounds), halved, pitted, and sliced
⅓ cup apricot preserves, warmed until melted down
2 tablespoons granulated sugar
1 tablespoon lemon juice

¼ teaspoon ground cinnamon
1½ tablespoons unsalted butter, melted and cooled
1 recipe Nut Crisp Topping (page 34), made with chopped almonds

Preheat the oven to 375 degrees. Butter a 9-inch oval ovenproof baking dish.

In a mixing bowl, toss the apricot slices with the preserves, granulated sugar, lemon juice, cinnamon, and melted butter. Spoon the fruit into the baking dish. Sprinkle the crisp topping over the fruit in an even layer.

Bake the crisp for 40 minutes, or until the apricots are tender and the topping is golden.

Apple Crisp with Currants

• 6 servings •

*W*hen just-picked apples appear at the farm market in huge baskets, it's time to make this simple crisp, so welcome on a brisk autumn day. In place of the superfine sugar, you can choose to sweeten the apples with ¼ cup warmed apple jelly, apple cider syrup (available at specialty food stores), or ¼ cup maple syrup.

¼ cup superfine sugar
½ teaspoon ground cinnamon
¼ teaspoon freshly grated nutmeg
5 cooking apples, such as
*   Stayman, Jonathan, or*
*   Rome Beauty (about 1⅔*
*   pounds), peeled, cored,*
*   and sliced*

1 tablespoon lemon juice
¼ cup moist, dried currants
1 recipe Nut Crisp Topping (page
*   34), made with walnuts*
*   or*
1 recipe Oatmeal Crisp Topping
*   (page 36)*

Preheat the oven to 375 degrees. Butter a 9-inch oval ovenproof baking dish.

In a mixing bowl, combine the superfine sugar, cinnamon, and nutmeg. Add the apples, lemon juice, and currants. Toss well. Spoon the fruit into the baking dish. Sprinkle the crisp topping over the fruit in an even layer.

Bake the crisp for 40 to 45 minutes, or until the apples are tender and the topping is golden.

Italian Prune Plum Crisp
with Dark Rum

• *6 servings* •

*O*ffer a pitcher of Nutmeg Custard Sauce (see page 80), flavored with a teaspoon of rum, for pouring alongside each helping of the crisp.

*16 Italian prune plums (about
    2 pounds), halved, pitted,
    and quartered
⅓ cup red currant jelly, warmed
    until melted down
2 tablespoons water*

*1½ tablespoons dark rum
2 tablespoons unsalted butter,
    melted and cooled
1 recipe Nut Crisp Topping (page
    34), made with walnuts*

Preheat the oven to 375 degrees. Butter a 9-inch oval ovenproof baking dish.

In a mixing bowl, toss the plum quarters with the jelly, water, rum, and butter. Spoon the fruit into the baking dish. Sprinkle the crisp topping over the fruit in an even layer.

Bake the crisp for 45 minutes, or until the plums are tender and the topping is golden.

Gingered Apple-Pear Crisp with Golden Raisins

• 6 servings •

*G*inger preserved in syrup, sweet and pungent, spices up the supple baked apples and pears.

3 cooking apples (about 1 pound), peeled, cored, and sliced	½ teaspoon ground cinnamon
	½ teaspoon ground ginger
	1 tablespoon lemon juice
3 pears (about 1 pound), peeled, cored, and sliced	1½ tablespoons chopped ginger preserved in syrup
⅓ cup apple jelly, warmed until melted down	3 tablespoons golden raisins
2 tablespoons honey	1 recipe Nut Crisp Topping (page 34), made with walnuts

Preheat the oven to 375 degrees. Butter a 9-inch oval ovenproof baking dish.

In a mixing bowl, toss the sliced apples and pears with the jelly, honey, cinnamon, ground ginger, lemon juice, preserved ginger, and raisins. Spoon the fruit into the baking dish. Sprinkle the crisp topping over the fruit in an even layer.

Bake the crisp for 45 minutes, or until the apples are tender and the topping is golden.

Mixed Berry Crisp

• *6 servings* •

*F*irm, ripe berries, tossed with sugar, spices, and just enough lemon peel to heighten their taste, create a superb crisp. Use the granola topping: it's extra crunchy and a good contrast to the softness of the baked berries.

3 cups blueberries, picked over
1 cup blackberries, picked over
1 cup black raspberries, picked over
⅓ cup plus 2¼ tablespoons superfine sugar blended with 2 teaspoons cornstarch, ¼ teaspoon freshly grated nutmeg, ¼ teaspoon ground cinnamon, and a pinch of ground allspice

2 teaspoons lemon juice
1 teaspoon grated lemon peel
1 recipe Granola Crisp Topping (page 35)

Preheat the oven to 375 degrees. Butter a 9-inch oval ovenproof baking dish.

In a mixing bowl, toss the blueberries, blackberries, and black raspberries with the superfine sugar-cornstarch-spice mixture, lemon juice, and lemon peel. Spoon the fruit into the baking dish. Sprinkle the crisp topping over the fruit in an even layer.

Bake the crisp for 40 to 45 minutes, or until the berries are bubbling and the topping is golden.

NOTE: If black raspberries are unavailable, increase the amount of blackberries to 2 cups and use ½ cup superfine sugar.

Orange-Blackberry Crisp

• *6 servings* •

*D*epending upon the tartness of the blackberries, you may wish to increase the amount of preserves to ¾ cup.

4 cups blackberries, picked over
½ cup blackberry preserves
2 teaspoons cornstarch blended
   with 1 tablespoon cold water
½ teaspoon ground allspice

2 teaspoons grated orange peel
1 tablespoon unsalted butter, melted
1 recipe Nut Crisp Topping (page
   34), made with walnuts

Preheat the oven to 375 degrees. Butter a 9-inch oval ovenproof baking dish.

In a mixing bowl, toss the blackberries with the preserves, cornstarch, allspice, orange peel, and butter. Spoon the fruit into the baking dish. Sprinkle the crisp topping over the fruit in an even layer.

Bake the crisp for 40 to 45 minutes, or until the blackberries are tender and the topping is golden.

Sour Cherry Crisp

• 6 servings •

Sour cherries make an unusually good filling for a fruit crisp. As the sour cherry season is short but plentiful, I freeze the whole (stemmed and unpitted) cherries in freezer-safe plastic bags and containers and use the supply in cobblers and crisps. Serve the crisp with whipped cream scented with a pinch of ground ginger.

4 cups sour cherries (about 2 pounds), pitted
¾ cup superfine sugar, or more to taste (depending upon the tartness of the fruit)
½ teaspoon ground ginger

1 tablespoon cornstarch blended with 3 tablespoons apple juice
2 tablespoons moist, dried currants
1 recipe Nut Crisp Topping (page 34), made with almonds or macadamia nuts

Preheat the oven to 375 degrees. Butter a 9-inch oval ovenproof baking dish.

In a mixing bowl, toss the cherries with the superfine sugar, ginger, cornstarch-juice mixture, and currants. Spoon the fruit into the baking dish. Sprinkle the crisp topping over the fruit in an even layer.

Bake the crisp for 40 to 45 minutes, or until the cherries are tender and the topping is golden.

Spiced Peach Crisp

• *6 servings* •

A glimmer of good bourbon, sprinkled over the peaches just before you blanket the fruit with the topping, makes this crisp memorable. Serve the crisp with the Honey-Vanilla Yogurt Sauce (page 79) or Softly Whipped Cream (page 78).

6 peaches (about 1½ pounds),
   peeled, pitted, and sliced
1 tablespoon lemon juice
2 tablespoons granulated sugar
   blended with ½ teaspoon
   ground cinnamon,
   ¼ teaspoon freshly grated
   nutmeg, ¼ teaspoon ground
   ginger, ⅛ teaspoon ground
   allspice, and 2 teaspoons
   cornstarch

2 tablespoons peach preserves
1 tablespoon bourbon
1 recipe Nut Crisp Topping (page
   34), made with almonds
   or
1 recipe Granola Crisp Topping
   (page 35)
   or
1 recipe Oatmeal Crisp Topping
   (page 36)

Preheat the oven to 375 degrees. Butter a 9-inch oval ovenproof baking dish.

In a mixing bowl, toss the sliced peaches with the lemon juice, granulated sugar-spice-cornstarch mixture, and preserves. Spoon the fruit into

the baking dish. Drizzle the bourbon over the fruit. Sprinkle the crisp topping over the fruit in an even layer.

Bake the crisp for 40 minutes, or until the peaches are tender and the topping is golden.

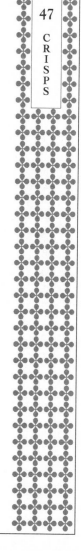

Red Plum Crisp

• *6 servings* •

A tablespoon of orange juice concentrate picks up the flavor of the sliced plums as they bake.

10 red plums (about 2 pounds), halved, pitted, and thickly sliced

¼ cup superfine sugar blended with 2 teaspoons cornstarch, ¼ teaspoon ground allspice, and ¾ teaspoon ground cinnamon

2 tablespoons thawed orange juice concentrate

1 recipe Nut Crisp Topping (page 34), made with walnuts
or
1 recipe Oatmeal Crisp Topping (page 36)
or
1 recipe Granola Crisp Topping (page 35)

Preheat the oven to 375 degrees. Butter a 9-inch oval ovenproof baking dish.

In a mixing bowl, toss the plums with the superfine sugar-cornstarch-spice mixture and orange juice concentrate. Spoon the fruit into the baking dish. Sprinkle the crisp topping over the fruit in an even layer.

Bake the crisp for 40 minutes, or until the plums are bubbly and tender and the topping is golden.

Pear-Mincemeat Crisp

• 6 servings •

*M*incemeat is one of those homemade enhancements that's easy to have simmering on the back burner while you go about doing other things in the kitchen or around the house. I keep it on hand for adding to pie fillings, puddings, and, of course, fruit crisps made with apples or pears.

*6 pears, peeled, cored, and
    sliced*
*½ cup Quick Dried Fruit
    Mincemeat (page 50)*
1 tablespoon maple syrup
2 teaspoons lemon juice

½ teaspoon grated lemon peel
*1 recipe Nut Crisp Topping (page
    34), made with walnuts*
or
*1 recipe Oatmeal Crisp Topping
    (page 36)*

Preheat the oven to 375 degrees. Butter a 9-inch oval ovenproof baking dish.

In a mixing bowl, toss the pears with the mincemeat, maple syrup, lemon juice, amd lemon peel. Spoon the fruit into the baking dish. Sprinkle the crisp topping over the fruit in an even layer.

Bake the crisp for 45 minutes, or until the pears are tender and the topping is golden.

Quick Dried Fruit Mincemeat

• *Makes about 1 quart* •

*M*incemeat made with a medley of chopped dried fruit, spices, and enough liquid to simmer the mixture to a delicate thickness is superb to keep in the refrigerator for embellishing desserts. Of all the dried fruit available, I love to use a combination of mangoes, apricots, pitted prunes, pears, peaches, golden raisins, and figs. You can use whatever is on hand in your pantry, keeping in mind that a diversity of fruit is what makes the finished mincemeat interesting and toothsome.

*4 cups coarsely chopped mixed
    dried fruit*
⅓ cup granulated sugar
2 tablespoons apple jelly
2 cups white grape juice
¼ cup bourbon or dark rum
1 cinnamon stick

*½ vanilla bean, split slightly to
    expose the seeds*
¼ teaspoon ground allspice
¼ teaspoon freshly grated nutmeg
¼ teaspoon ground ginger
½ cup chopped walnuts (optional)

Place the fruit in a 6- to 8-quart nonreactive casserole (preferably enameled cast iron). Stir in the granulated sugar and apple jelly. Pour over the grape juice and liquor. Bury the cinnamon stick and vanilla bean in the mixture and let stand for 20 minutes. Stir in the allspice, nutmeg, and ginger. Bring the mixture to a boil. Simmer the mincemeat, covered, for 20 minutes. Uncover and simmer until the fruit is tender and the mixture is lightly thickened, about 10 to 15 minutes longer. Stir in the walnuts, if you are using them.

Cool the mincemeat completely. Spoon into a sturdy storage container, cover tightly, and refrigerate. The mincemeat will keep in the refrigerator for 2 months.

Deep-Dish Pies

A deep-dish pie, with its generous measure of fruit hidden beneath a flaky crust, joins the market's best with the fine art of American pie making. Sliced fruit, seasoned and piled high, bakes succulently under a tender dough, creating a dessert that is both basic and lavish.

To cover a deep-dish pie, I now like to use a pie dough made with almost equal quantities of unsalted butter and solid shortening, an egg yolk for richness, granulated sugar, and ice-cold milk mixed with a hint of vanilla extract. The milk, as opposed to water, builds a crust with a richer flake. The blend of butter (for flavor) and shortening (for texture) creates a crust that is full of flavor, yet tender. And the sugar helps to give the crust a (sometimes elusive) golden-hued cast.

The making of a deep-dish pie is straightforward, once you have a portion of pastry dough ready to go, and a bowl of sliced fruit (or berries, picked over), sugared and spiced, that has been bound moderately with a thickener. Fruit needs a binding agent of some sort so that the baked filling finishes with body and substance. (For more information on the importance of thickeners, please see page 4.)

The deep-dish pie pan I use is oval, ovenproof porcelain, about 3 ½ inches deep. It has a wide rim that serves as both a sturdy anchor for the weight of the top crust and as a good space to use for making handsome fluted or crimped borders. A deep metal pie pan (without a perforated bottom) can be used in place of the porcelain variety.

Deep-Dish Pie Crust

• Enough pie dough to cover a 9- or 10-inch deep-dish pie pan •

This recipe is a variation of the recipe for "Flaky Pie Crust for a Double-Crust Pie" that I published in *Country Pies: A Seasonal Sampler* (New York: Harper & Row, 1988). The general method for mixing, rolling, and forming the dough into a top crust also comes from various sections in the chapter titled "About Baking Country Pies."

The formula you have here creates a generous amount of dough for just a top crust, but I now find that it is much easier to work with a little more dough when you are covering a large mound of fruit. The extra snippets of dough can be used for decorating the top of the pie, if you wish.

2 cups all-purpose flour
¼ teaspoon salt
6 tablespoons cold unsalted but-
    ter, cut into small chunks
5 tablespoons frozen solid
    shortening, cut into small
    chunks

1 tablespoon granulated sugar
1 extra-large egg yolk
¼ teaspoon vanilla extract
3 tablespoons cold milk

FOR FINISHING THE TOP CRUST JUST BEFORE BAKING:

Ice-cold water, for brushing the
    top of the pie

About 2 teaspoons granulated
    sugar, for sprinkling

Preparing the Pie Crust

Combine the flour and salt in a large mixing bowl. Scatter over the butter and shortening and cut up the fat, using 2 round-bladed knives, until it is reduced to small pieces. Continue to blend the fat into the flour, using your fingertips: Crumble it between your fingertips by dipping down and up into the mixture. This combination will look pebbly. Lightly stir in the 1 tablespoon granulated sugar. Blend together the egg yolk, vanilla, and milk in a small bowl. Pour over the flour mixture, and mix quickly to form a dough.

Transfer the dough to a large sheet of wax paper and press into a flat cake. Wrap it and refrigerate for 15 minutes.

Rolling Out the Pie Crust

Roll out the dough between two sheets of wax paper. It should be a scant ¼ inch thick. Carefully lift the dough onto a cookie sheet and chill for 30 minutes. (At this point, the rolled-out length of dough may be refrigerated, covered in plastic wrap, for up to 2 days.)

Covering the Mound of Fruit with the Pie Crust

At this point, the pie dish should be filled with the fruit filling.

Peel away one sheet of wax paper from the sheet of dough. Cut strips of dough about ⅓ inch thick from the outside of the circle of dough. Lightly brush the rim of a 9- or 10-inch (depending on the recipe) ovenproof oval or round deep-dish pie pan with ice water. Press on the strips of dough and brush lightly with ice water. Place the pie crust over the filling by inverting the circle of dough over the fruit. Quickly but care-

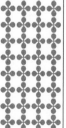

(continued)

fully peel away the sheet of wax paper. Press the top crust onto the dough-lined rim. Carefully cut away the overhang of dough with a sharp paring knife. Flute or crimp the edges decoratively. Refrigerate the pie for 10 minutes.

Just before baking, lightly brush the top of the pie with the ice-cold water and sprinkle with the granulated sugar. Bake as directed.

Deep-Dish Apple Pie with Currants and Spices

• *6 servings* •

*F*or a pie filling with the best flavor and texture, use firm and sweet-tart apples, such as Macintosh, Jonathan, or Rome Beauty.

½ cup granulated sugar

¼ cup light brown sugar

2¾ teaspoons cornstarch

1 teaspoon ground cinnamon

¼ teaspoon freshly grated nutmeg

⅛ teaspoon ground cardamom

*6 cooking apples (about 2
    pounds), peeled, cored,
    and sliced*

1 tablespoon lemon juice

2 tablespoons moist, dried currants

*1 recipe Deep-Dish Pie Crust
    (page 54), prepared through
    "Rolling Out the Pie Crust"
    (page 55)*

Preheat the oven to 425 degrees. Have a 10-inch deep-dish pie pan at hand.

In a mixing bowl, combine the granulated sugar, light brown sugar, cornstarch, cinnamon, nutmeg, and cardamom. Add the apple slices, lemon juice, and currants. Toss the fruit and the sugar mixture together lightly but thoroughly. Spoon the fruit into the pie dish, mounding it as you go.

Cover the fruit with the prepared pie dough, following the directions on page 55, "Covering the Mound of Fruit with the Pie Crust." Cut a few steam vents in the crust with a small, sharp knife.

Bake the pie for 10 minutes, reduce the oven temperature to 350 degrees, and continue baking for 40 to 45 minutes longer, or until the crust is golden and the fruit is tender.

Deep-Dish Peach Pie with Glazed Apricots and Walnuts

• *6 servings* •

A handful of diced, glazed apricots adds a sweet and tangy edge to this pie.

¾ cup plus 1 tablespoon granulated sugar
1 tablespoon cornstarch
¼ teaspoon ground cinnamon
¼ teaspoon ground ginger
¼ teaspoon ground allspice
8 peaches (about 2 pounds), peeled, pitted, and sliced

⅓ cup diced glazed apricots (about 3)
⅓ cup chopped walnuts, lightly toasted
1 recipe Deep-Dish Pie Crust (page 54), prepared through "Rolling Out the Pie Crust" (page 55)

Preheat the oven to 425 degrees. Have a 10-inch deep-dish pie pan at hand.

In a mixing bowl, combine the granulated sugar, cornstarch, cinnamon, ginger, and allspice. Add the peach slices, apricots, and walnuts. Toss the fruit and the sugar mixture together lightly but thoroughly. Spoon the fruit into the pie dish, mounding it as you go.

Cover the fruit with the prepared pie dough, following the directions on page 55, "Covering the Mound of Fruit with the Pie Crust." Cut a few steam vents in the crust with a small, sharp knife.

Bake the pie for 10 minutes, reduce the oven temperature to 350 degrees, and continue baking for 40 to 45 minutes longer, or until the crust is golden and the fruit is tender.

Deep-Dish Peach-Blackberry Pie

• *6 servings* •

$\mathcal{M}$ixed together, peaches and blackberries make a succulent pie. A tablespoon or two of blackberry jam, if on hand, intensifies the taste of the filling.

1 cup granulated sugar
2 tablespoons all-purpose flour
½ teaspoon freshly grated nutmeg
6 peaches (about 1½ pounds),
    peeled, pitted, and sliced
2 cups blackberries, picked over

1 tablespoon unsalted butter, cut
    into bits
1 recipe Deep-Dish Pie Crust
    (page 54), prepared through
    "Rolling Out the Pie Crust"
    (page 55)

Preheat the oven to 425 degrees. Have a 10-inch deep-dish pie pan at hand.

In a mixing bowl, combine the granulated sugar, flour, and nutmeg. Add the peach slices and blackberries. Toss the fruit and the sugar mixture together lightly but thoroughly. Spoon the fruit into the pie dish, mounding it as you go. Dot the top of the fruit with the bits of butter.

Cover the fruit with the prepared pie dough, following the directions on page 55, "Covering the Mound of Fruit with the Pie Crust." Cut a few steam vents in the crust with a small, sharp knife.

Bake the pie for 10 minutes, reduce the oven temperature to 350 degrees, and continue baking for 40 minutes longer, or until the crust is golden and the fruit is tender.

Deep-Dish Lemon-Blueberry Pie

• 6 servings •

Chopped glazed lemon peel, if you have some on hand, can be added to the filling along with the grated peel and juice.

1 cup granulated sugar	*1 tablespoon unsalted butter, cut*
2 tablespoons cornstarch	*into bits*
½ teaspoon freshly grated nutmeg	*1 recipe Deep-Dish Pie Crust*
5 cups blueberries, picked over	*(page 54), prepared through*
1 tablespoon lemon juice	*"Rolling Out the Pie Crust"*
1 teaspoon grated lemon peel	*(page 55)*

Preheat the oven to 425 degrees. Have a 10-inch deep-dish pie pan at hand.

In a mixing bowl, combine the granulated sugar, cornstarch, and nutmeg. Add the blueberries, lemon juice, and lemon peel. Toss the fruit and the sugar mixture together lightly but thoroughly. Spoon the fruit into the pie dish, mounding it as you go. Dot the top of the fruit with the bits of butter.

Cover the fruit with the prepared pie dough, following the directions on page 55, "Covering the Mound of Fruit with the Pie Crust." Cut a few steam vents in the crust with a small, sharp knife.

Bake the pie for 10 minutes, reduce the oven temperature to 350 degrees, and continue baking for 40 minutes longer, or until the crust is golden and the fruit is tender.

Deep-Dish Cherry Pie

• *6 servings* •

$\mathcal{S}$ince a wisp of almond extract flavors the cherries, you can also mix a sprinkling of slivered almonds (about ¼ cup) into the fruit, sugar, and spice mixture.

¾ cup granulated sugar
2 tablespoons all-purpose flour
½ teaspoon ground cinnamon
¼ teaspoon ground ginger
5½ cups cherries (about 2½
    pounds), pitted
½ teaspoon almond extract

1 tablespoon unsalted butter, cut
    into bits
1 recipe Deep-Dish Pie Crust
    (page 54), prepared through
    "Rolling Out the Pie Crust"
    (page 55)

Preheat the oven to 425 degrees. Have a 10-inch deep-dish pie pan at hand.

In a mixing bowl, combine the granulated sugar, flour, cinnamon, and ginger. Add the cherries and almond extract. Toss the fruit and the sugar mixture together lightly but thoroughly. Spoon the fruit into the pie dish, mounding it as you go. Dot the top of the fruit with the bits of butter.

Cover the fruit with the prepared pie dough, following the directions on page 55, "Covering the Mound of Fruit with the Pie Crust." Cut a few steam vents in the crust with a small, sharp knife.

Bake the pie for 10 minutes, reduce the oven temperature to 350 degrees, and continue baking for 40 to 45 minutes longer, or until the crust is golden and the fruit is tender.

VARIATION

For *Deep-Dish Sour Cherry Pie*, use sour cherries in place of the sweet cherries and increase the amount of granulated sugar to 1¼ cups.

Deep-Dish Red Plum Pie

• *6 servings* •

A tablespoon of dark rum would add a keen kick to the filling. If you are including the rum, replace ¼ cup of the granulated sugar with dark or light brown sugar.

¾ cup granulated sugar
1¾ tablespoons cornstarch
½ teaspoon ground cinnamon
14 red plums (about 2⅓
   pounds), halved, pitted,
   and sliced

1 tablespoon unsalted butter,
   cut into bits
1 recipe Deep-Dish Pie Crust
   (page 54), prepared through
   "Rolling Out the Pie Crust"
   (page 55)

Preheat the oven to 425 degrees. Have a 10-inch deep-dish pie pan at hand.

In a mixing bowl, combine the granulated sugar, cornstarch, and cinnamon. Add the plum slices. Toss the fruit and the sugar mixture together lightly but thoroughly. Spoon the fruit into the pie dish, mounding it as you go. Dot the top of the fruit with the bits of butter.

Cover the fruit with the prepared pie dough, following the directions on page 55, "Covering the Mound of Fruit with the Pie Crust." Cut a few steam vents in the crust with a small, sharp knife.

Bake the pie for 10 minutes, reduce the oven temperature to 350 degrees, and continue baking for 40 minutes longer, or until the crust is golden and the fruit is tender.

Deep-Dish Blueberry-Nectarine Pie

• 6 servings •

*T*wo tablespoons of dried blueberries, macerated in 2 tablespoons of light rum or white grape juice, can be blended into the filling along with the fresh berries and sliced nectarines.

1 cup granulated sugar
2 tablespoons cornstarch
½ teaspoon ground cinnamon
¼ teaspoon ground allspice
8 nectarines (about 2 pounds),
    halved, pitted, and sliced

1¼ cups blueberries, picked over
1 recipe Deep-Dish Pie Crust
    (page 54), prepared through
    "Rolling Out the Pie Crust"
    (page 55)

Preheat the oven to 425 degrees. Have a 10-inch deep-dish pie pan at hand.

In a mixing bowl, combine the granulated sugar, cornstarch, cinnamon, and allspice. Add the nectarine slices and blueberries. Toss the fruit and the sugar mixture together lightly but thoroughly. Spoon the fruit into the pie dish, mounding it as you go.

Cover the fruit with the prepared pie dough, following the directions on page 55, "Covering the Mound of Fruit with the Pie Crust." Cut a few steam vents in the crust with a small, sharp knife.

Bake the pie for 10 minutes, reduce the oven temperature to 350 degrees, and continue baking for 40 to 45 minutes longer, or until the crust is golden and the fruit is tender.

Deep-Dish Strawberry-Rhubarb Pie

• *6 servings* •

A little trick for uplifting the flavor of this classic pie filling is to spoon 2 tablespoons of warm red currant jelly through the fruit filling just before turning it into the pie dish.

1¼ cups granulated sugar
3 tablespoons cornstarch
½ teaspoon grated lemon peel
3 pints strawberries, hulled
4 stalks trimmed and sliced
    rhubarb (about 2 cups)

2 tablespoons red currant jelly,
    warmed slightly to melt down
1 recipe Deep-Dish Pie Crust
    (page 54), prepared through
    "Rolling Out the Pie Crust"
    (page 55)

Preheat the oven to 425 degrees. Have a 10-inch deep-dish pie pan at hand.

In a mixing bowl, combine the granulated sugar and cornstarch. Add the lemon peel, strawberries, and rhubarb. Toss the fruit and the sugar mixture together lightly but thoroughly. Toss again with the red currant jelly. Spoon the fruit into the pie dish, mounding it as you go.

Cover the fruit with the prepared pie dough, following the directions on page 55, "Covering the Mound of Fruit with the Pie Crust." Cut a few steam vents in the crust with a small, sharp knife.

Bake the pie for 10 minutes, reduce the oven temperature to 350 degrees, and continue baking for 45 minutes longer, or until the crust is golden and the fruit is tender.

NOTE: At the market, rhubarb is generally sold trimmed of its leaves, which are poisonous and should never be consumed or used in baking.

Deep-Dish Pear Pie with Dried Cranberries

• *6 servings* •

*T*he dried cranberries are a chewy contrast to the supple baked pear slices.

¾ cup granulated sugar
1 tablespoon flour
½ teaspoon ground ginger
¼ teaspoon freshly grated nutmeg
7 pears (about 2⅓ pounds),
 peeled, halved, cored, and
 sliced
2 tablespoons dried cranberries,
 coarsely chopped if large

2 teaspoons lemon juice
1 tablespoon unsalted butter,
 cut into bits
1 recipe Deep-Dish Pie Crust
 (page 54), prepared through
 "Rolling Out the Pie Crust"
 (page 55)

Preheat the oven to 425 degrees. Have a 10-inch deep-dish pie pan at hand.

In a mixing bowl, combine the granulated sugar, flour, ginger, and nutmeg. Add the pear slices, cranberries, and lemon juice. Toss the fruit and the sugar mixture together lightly but thoroughly. Spoon the fruit into the pie dish, mounding it as you go. Dot the top of the fruit with the bits of butter.

Cover the fruit with the prepared pie dough, following the directions on page 55, "Covering the Mound of Fruit with the Pie Crust." Cut a few steam vents in the crust with a small, sharp knife.

Bake the pie for 10 minutes, reduce the oven temperature to 350 degrees, and continue baking for 45 minutes longer, or until the crust is golden and the fruit is tender.

Deep-Dish Mixed Berry Pie

• *6 servings* •

A berry pie is the embodiment of summer baking. And is there anything quite like the aroma released from this pie when you break into the top crust with a spoon?

1¼ cups granulated sugar
3 tablespoons cornstarch
½ teaspoon ground cinnamon
¼ teaspoon ground allspice
3½ cups blueberries, picked over
3 cups blackberries, picked over
2 cups strawberries, hulled

1 teaspoon grated lemon peel
1 tablespoon unsalted butter, cut
   into bits
1 recipe Deep-Dish Pie Crust
   (page 54), prepared through
   "Rolling Out the Pie Crust"
   (page 55)

Preheat the oven to 425 degrees. Have a 10-inch deep-dish pie pan at hand.

In a mixing bowl, combine the granulated sugar, cornstarch, cinnamon, and allspice. Add the blueberries, blackberries, strawberries, and lemon peel. Toss the fruit and the sugar mixture together lightly but thoroughly. Spoon the fruit into the pie dish, mounding it as you go. Dot the top of the fruit with the bits of butter.

Cover the fruit with the prepared pie dough, following the directions on page 55, "Covering the Mound of Fruit with the Pie Crust." Cut a few steam vents in the crust with a small, sharp knife.

Bake the pie for 10 minutes, reduce the oven temperature to 350 degrees, and continue baking for 40 to 45 minutes longer, or until the crust is golden and the fruit is tender.

Deep-Dish Rhubarb Pie

• *6 servings* •

To mellow the bouquet of a pie made entirely of rhubarb, add orange juice concentrate and grated orange peel to the filling.

1½ cups granulated sugar
2 tablespoons all-purpose flour
¼ teaspoon ground allspice
9 stalks trimmed and sliced
   rhubarb (about 5 cups)
2 tablespoons thawed orange
   juice concentrate

1½ teaspoons grated orange peel
1 tablespoon unsalted butter, cut
   into bits
1 recipe Deep-Dish Pie Crust
   (page 54), prepared through
   "Rolling Out the Pie Crust"
   (page 55)

Preheat the oven to 425 degrees. Have a 10-inch deep-dish pie pan at hand.

In a mixing bowl, combine the granulated sugar, flour, and allspice. Add the rhubarb slices. Toss the fruit and the sugar mixture together with the orange juice concentrate and orange peel. Spoon the fruit into the pie dish, mounding it as you go. Dot the top of the fruit with the bits of butter.

Cover the fruit with the prepared pie dough, following the directions on page 55, "Covering the Mound of Fruit with the Pie Crust." Cut a few steam vents in the crust with a small, sharp knife.

Bake the pie for 10 minutes, reduce the oven temperature to 350 degrees, and continue baking for 45 to 50 minutes longer, or until the crust is golden and the fruit is tender.

NOTE: At the market, rhubarb is generally sold trimmed of its leaves, which are poisonous and should never be consumed or used in baking.

Deep-Dish Apricot Pie with Spices

• *6 servings* •

*T*wo tablespoons of apricot preserves added to the filling brings out the soft, perfumelike quality of the fresh fruit.

¾ cup plus 2 tablespoons
    granulated sugar
1 tablespoon cornstarch
¼ teaspoon ground cinnamon
¼ teaspoon ground ginger
¼ teaspoon freshly grated nutmeg
¼ teaspoon ground allspice
15 apricots (about 2¼ pounds),
    halved, pitted, and thickly
    sliced

1 teaspoon lemon juice
½ teaspoon grated lemon peel
2 tablespoons apricot preserves
1 tablespoon unsalted butter, cut
    into bits
1 recipe Deep-Dish Pie Crust
    (page 54), prepared through
    "Rolling Out the Pie Crust"
    (page 55)

Preheat the oven to 425 degrees. Have a 10-inch deep-dish pie pan at hand.

In a mixing bowl, combine the granulated sugar, cornstarch, cinnamon, ginger, nutmeg, and allspice. Add the apricot slices, lemon juice, lemon peel, and apricot preserves. Toss the fruit and the sugar mixture together lightly but thoroughly. Spoon the fruit into the pie dish, mounding it as you go. Dot the top of the fruit with the bits of butter.

Cover the fruit with the prepared pie dough, following the directions on page 55, "Covering the Mound of Fruit with the Pie Crust." Cut a few steam vents in the crust with a small, sharp knife.

Bake the pie for 10 minutes, reduce the oven temperature to 350 degrees, and continue baking for 45 minutes longer, or until the crust is golden and the fruit is tender.

Deep-Dish Apricot, Peach, and Nectarine Pie

• *6 servings* •

*F*reshly grated orange peel brings out all the rounded flavors in this medley of fruit. For extra flavor, add a tablespoon of apricot schnapps to the filling and several chopped glazed apricots or a tablespoon of diced candied orange peel.

1 cup granulated sugar
2 tablespoons all-purpose flour
½ teaspoon freshly grated nutmeg
¼ teaspoon ground cinnamon
4 peaches (about 1 pound), peeled, halved, pitted, and sliced
8 apricots (about 1 pound), halved, pitted, and sliced

3 nectarines (about ¾ pound), halved, pitted and sliced
1 teaspoon grated orange peel
1 recipe Deep-Dish Pie Crust (page 54), prepared through "Rolling Out the Pie Crust" (page 55)

Preheat the oven to 425 degrees. Have a 10-inch deep-dish pie pan at hand.

In a mixing bowl, combine the granulated sugar, flour, nutmeg, and cinnamon. Add the peaches, apricots, nectarines, and orange peel. Toss the fruit and the sugar mixture together lightly but thoroughly. Spoon the fruit into the pie dish, mounding it as you go.

Cover the fruit with the prepared pie dough, following the directions on page 55, "Covering the Mound of Fruit with the Pie Crust." Cut a few steam vents in the crust with a small, sharp knife.

Bake the pie for 10 minutes, reduce the oven temperature to 350 degrees, and continue baking for 45 minutes longer, or until the crust is golden and the fruit is tender.

A Spoonful of Sauce

As a sauce, a stream of pure heavy cream can be a simple and delicious no-cook accompaniment to a warm fruit dessert. With a few more ingredients and, perhaps, a saucepan or a whisk, other textures and flavors are ready to be concocted and quickly turn any cobbler, crisp, or pie into a company treat.

Softly Whipped Cream

• *About 2¾ cups* •

Puffy mounds of whipped cream provide just the right creamy lightness for a helping of fruit crisp or deep-dish pie.

1¼ cups cold heavy cream

2½ tablespoons sifted confectioners' sugar

Pour the cream into a chilled bowl. Whip the cream until it barely begins to mound. Add the confectioners' sugar and continue whipping until very soft peaks are formed. The cream should *just* hold its shape in a spoon. Use immediately.

Honey-Vanilla Yogurt Sauce

• *A generous 1½ cups* •

*T*his sauce is light and tangy, and is faintly perfumed with vanilla extract and the scraped seeds from a small section of vanilla bean. It serves as a delicious addition to the variety of baked desserts in this book, most particularly those made with the soft fruits of summer—berries, peaches, nectarines, and the like.

1½ cups plain yogurt (low-fat can be substituted)
1 teaspoon vanilla extract

Seed scrapings from a 1½-inch piece of vanilla bean
2 tablespoons honey, or to taste

In a mixing bowl, stir together the yogurt, vanilla extract, vanilla bean–seed scrapings, and honey. Use the sauce immediately, or cover and refrigerate for up to 2 days. Restir the blended sauce just before using.

Nutmeg Custard Sauce

• *About 1¼ cups* •

*T*his sauce is a perfect grace note to almost any of the sweets in this book. The custard is spiked with freshly grated nutmeg rather than the preground, bottled variety. Whole nutmegs are easy to scrape over the fine holes of a four-sided box grater. A grater especially designed for reducing the whole spice to a powder is a useful kitchen tool and, for easy storage, has a metal or plastic pocket on its underside to hold the nutmegs.

1 cup plus 2 tablespoons milk
½ cup heavy cream
2½ tablespoons granulated sugar
  blended with ¼ teaspoon
  freshly grated nutmeg and a
  pinch of salt

5 extra-large egg yolks
½ teaspoon vanilla extract

Scald the milk and cream; remove from the heat. Place sugar-nutmeg-salt blend and the egg yolks in a heavy saucepan (preferably enameled cast iron) and whisk for 3 to 4 minutes, or until creamy in texture and well blended. The mixture will thicken slightly. Add a few tablespoons of the scalded mixture to the egg yolk and sugar mixture, then stir in the remaining liquid in a slow, steady stream.

Place the saucepan over low heat and cook, stirring with a wooden spoon, until the sauce coats the back of the spoon and is about the consistency of good, preservative-free heavy cream. A little patience is needed here: The mixture should take about 10 to 12 minutes to thicken to a silky mass. (If the heat is raised to speed up the process, the egg yolks will form small curdles, thus spoiling the sauce.) Remove the saucepan from the heat, blend the vanilla extract into the thickened sauce, and cool for 1 minute, stirring occasionally.

Strain the sauce into a heatproof container. (I use a fine-meshed stainless steel sieve for this process.) Place a piece of plastic wrap directly on the surface of the sauce to prevent a skin from forming. Cool completely, cover, and refrigerate. The sauce will keep in the refrigerator for up to 2 days.

NOTE: Upon standing in the refrigerator, the sauce thickens somewhat. Thin it out with milk, adding it a teaspoon at a time, taking care to avoid diluting it; the sauce should puddle on a dessert plate.

Index